Cackling In The White House

By Sean Seville

The Pisser Presidential Trilogy

Part I Our First Orange President

Part II Mumbling Fool: An American President

Part III Cackling In The White House

Table of Contents

PBJ presents former President, Ronald Dump

Panel Of Black Journalists

An annual convention has taken place named the "PB and J" Panel Of Black Journalists. This year three esteemed members of the press: Senior Congressional Correspondent Maple Escrott, News Anchor Sarah Autner, and Political Reporter Nadja Robar moderated an interview with a very special guest indeed. There was a combined attendance of approximately two hundred reporters among the varied spectatorship. The rented hall for this event had reached full capacity. On stage there were four chairs.

Three for the moderators and one for... Extraordinarily loud and whistling sounds rang throughout the hall, during an unexpected display of pyrotechnics. Once that stopped, the music of a popular singer from the 1980s began to play over the loud speakers. Suddenly a man with an orange complexion came out on stage while performing "The Moonwalk". As soon as he was in close proximity of the moderators he spun around.

Then he grabbed his crotch while gyrating his hips four or five times before spinning around again. It was at this very moment that the music ceased, and so did the antics of this citrus colored individual. The act was met with just as much applause as there were boos. The three women shook hands with their guest before everyone on stage took a seat. The special guest that was to be interviewed was none other than the former President Of The United States, Ronald T. Dump.

Maple Escrott immediately addressed the ex- commander in chief regarding past allegations he made that former P.O.T.U.S, Harmack Labamba was not an actual U.S citizen. Questions were also raised about his refusal to rent to rent to blacks when he used to own rental properties and various other forms of real estate,

Dump spending time with former and current members of the Ku Klux Klan, and allegedly chuckling while watching replays of video footage from high profile cases that depict cops killing black people. This line of inquiries angered Dump. He felt that Escrott was nasty and she had a nasty attitude.

"I don't remember the last time I was spoken to in such a nasty manner," Dump remarked. "You're not qualified to ask me these kind of questions. Instead, you should be at a drive thru window asking me, 'Would you like fries with your burger?' Dump said.

Naturally the reporters and vast amount of onlookers found these comments to be appalling. Maple Escrott smirked before speaking.

"Due to your tumultuous past with the black community, how can you ever expect to garner their votes?" Maple asked.

Dump thought of Escrott as an irritant. He displayed a deep rooted frown that couldn't be more apparent.

"Listen, I love the black population and they love me," Dump replied. Grumbles and muttering came from the crowd.

Ronald continued on, "I plan to eliminate the threat of illegal immigrants taking black jobs. If I want to have my car washed, an African American has every right to do it. And while I'm out on the golf course the black man may not be able to play but he can sure as hell caddie for me," Dump said.

Members of the crowd heckled Ronald for several minutes before they finally stopped and the interview could continue.

Maple uncrossed her legs before leaning forward.

"You have made a series of false claims against Vice President Jacqueline

Barris and copious disparaging remarks. Is this any different than how you've treated your rivals in the past?" Escrott asked.

Dump sat there with a smug appearance on his face.

does this work exactly? Personally, I don't get it but she is welcome to serve me some of that naan bread and samosas. I heard there are videos out there of her cooking that stuff. Her family probably owns a restaurant somewhere," Dump said.

This nonsense carried on for an additional thirty minutes. Maple Escrott and her colleagues persistently asked the former president questions in an attempt to cause the man to hang himself with his own words. What the congressional correspondent and many other adversaries of the ex- president fail to realize is that no matter what he says or does, Ronald T. Dump will never face any consequences. "The Teflon Ron" is seemingly invincible.

fradonnia is Currently asleep.
Dump Sneaks away to make
a late night, long distance phone call.

What Happens In Vegas... Get The Hell Out Of Vegas

Bright lights of the big city. Here we are at long last. V.P. Jacqueline Barris has acquired enough pledged delegate votes from her political party to become the presumptive presidential nominee. Jacqueline's desire was to take a couple of days off before returning to the campaign trail.

Las Vegas seemed to be the appropriate place for leisure.

The Tonokee is arguably the largest casino in the city. The Vice President asked her assistant, Megan to book a suite for a two night stay. Megan stayed in a room that was halfway down the hall, and a couple of secret service men were stationed next door. Barris could not stand to remain bored in such a lively town. Jacqueline's campaign staff warned her not to engage in any of her typical hijinks.

It is of the utmost importance that Jacqueline would refrain from creating any embarrassing scenes, and to conduct herself in a professional manner.

Ultimately, Jacqueline couldn't resist giving into her inherent impulses. She reached underneath the pillow on her bed and pulled out a 9mm Beretta.

This was subsequent to placing a ski mask over her face. Barris grabbed one of her pillow cases before storming out of her room.

The secret service men were performing surveillance on the Vice President's suite. As soon as Jacqueline began to traverse the hallways, the secret service men followed suit. Both James and Gill worked in this line duty for over fifteen years. Barris is one of the most difficult clients that they ever had, but they were determined to fulfill their duties regardless of the consequences.

After taking the elevator down to the first floor, Jacqueline marched hastily toward the cashier's cage with James and Gill following closely behind. Once Barris reached her destination, she fired a couple of rounds into the air. Patrons screamed and struggled not to panic. Security chose not to intervene. They knew exactly who it was underneath the mask.

Jacqueline pointed her gun at the cashier while most

of the patrons began to flee the scene. Barris read the name pin on the cashier's shirt.

"Ha, ha, ha, ha. Hello there, Reba. Do you want to help out by giving me all of your god damn money?!" Jacqueline asked.

The cashier shook her head.

"No ma'am. I'm standing behind bullet proof glass. Your bullets won't hurt me," Reba replied.

Jacqueline laughed once again while reaching her gun through a small open space located underneath the glass.

"Now unless you want to go to the hospital with a severe tummy ache, I suggest that you give me the money," Jacqueline said.

Without a moment to spare, the cashier dumped $30,000 worth of casino chips in front of the Vice President.

"Who the hell said, I wanted chips?!" Barris asked.

Then she shrugged her shoulders and handed the pillowcase to Gill. "Load it up," Jacqueline said.

The secret service man gave a nod.

Yes, Madam Vice President," Gill said.

At this juncture the Casino was practically vacant. Only ten percent of the dealers remained standing by their respective tables, trembling in fear.

Barris hurried over to the black jack table. She pointed her gun and demanded some cards. The dealer did what was in his best interest and dealt the Vice President a couple of cards from the deck.

Jacqueline had 14. "Hit me!" She exclaimed.

Then Barris had 20 "Hit me again," she said.

The dealer sighed, "I don't think you know how this game works," he said.

Jacqueline pulled off her ski mask.

"Damn this thing is way too hot," the Vice President said. The dealer pretended to be in a total state of shock. "You're Jacqueline Barris," he said.

Then Barris proceeded in shooting the dealer directly in the throat. A thin stream of blood flowed outward, similar to a water fountain. The man died before hitting the floor. The secret service men approached Jacqueline from behind.

"Twenty one!" Jacqueline exclaimed. "Ha, ha, ha, ha, ha, ha! I didn't want to do it but he recognized me," she said. James cleared his throat.

"With all due respect, ma'am. He would not have recognized you if you didn't remove your mask," James said.

After shooting a few more people, Barris and the secret service headed toward the lounge. The Vice President wished to take in a show. Sailor Queef is currently the biggest pop star in the world, and she has a six month residency at the Tonokee Casino. The lounge happened to be full of patrons. No one there paid any attention to the barrage of gunshots or commotion that had taken place only minutes prior.

They all thought it was part of a planned act. It was time for the show to begin. The lights dimmed as Sailor Queef walked out on to the stage. Her elegant white dress reached all the way down to her ankles. The pop star wore three inch tall high heels.

Her blonde hair flowed like a waterfall. She began to sing one of her latest singles. Some time elapsed since the beginning of the show. Four songs into the performance and the Vice President couldn't bear it any longer. Sailor screeched her way through some of her top hits.

Jacqueline knew that the youth looked up to Queef as a role model. Barris stood up from her seat with gun in hand.

"For all the little girls out there, you can do better," Jacqueline said.

Then she fired six to nine rounds at the beloved pop star. Patrons screamed as they fled the lounge in haste. The bullets hit several vital organs. Sailor bled out quickly. She queefed as she took her last breath.

The Vice President glanced at the secret service men.

"Ha, ha, ha, ha. Well boys, I think it's time to check out," Jacqueline said.

Time To Get Presidential

Allow us to give some well deserved applause. A few weeks have passed and she is no longer presumptive. Jacqueline Barris has officially become the presidential nominee for her political party. Cross country touring and speaking to the American people within their natural habitats will now be an absolute necessity. Barris' staff had a notion to suggest.

They wanted Jacqueline to visit a university in an attempt to appeal to younger voters. Barris concurred with her staff's sentiment. Instead of traveling to her own Alma Mater, a decision was made that it would be more beneficial for Barris to stop by some college grounds that she never stepped foot on before. Her following destination is Bumford University. Once Jacqueline arrived she became ecstatic.

After speaking to a crowd of exuberant students, Barris inquired as to which sorority house on campus is the most popular. Soon she learned that Anogio Podi held the title. Hours later, the night sky presented itself upon the university campus.

An exclusive party was now in progress at that same sorority, and Jacqueline had every intention of attending.

After getting dressed for such an occasion Barris had several secret service men accompany her to the gathering. They brought a couple of beer kegs with them. Once the Vice President arrived the festivities became much more lively. One of the girls was sliding down a stripper pole that had been installed in the living room. Barris ordered one of her men to remove the young woman. The girl was grabbed by her neck and then thrown down onto the floor.

Jacqueline began working the pole like a pro. Several people recorded video footage of the VP at her raunchiest. Those same individuals had their phones confiscated and then destroyed by the Secret Service.

Barris decided to play Truth Or Dare with some of the girls.

One person named Daisy accepted a "Dare". Jacqueline ordered the young woman to give her best friend Shania a rim job. Eating ass is not part of a nutritious breakfast, lunch, or dinner but the mere thought amused

Jacqueline very much. A man from the secret service held a gun against Daisy's head after she refused. Barris shrugged her shoulders.

"You could have chosen, Truth, Jacqueline said.

All of the other girls that were participating in the game were horrified while they observed Daisy eating as if she were a cat lapping milk from a bowl. Most of the sorority sisters were engrossed in either dancing, talking, or drinking heavily. The Vice President received a text message that she read with glee. Then she vehemently announced the arrival of her running mate, Jim Mozz.

Politically, Mozz is a progressive governor from Minnesota. His intrinsic amiable qualities lead him to passionately fight for his fellow man (and woman) with an ambitious agenda that include tax cuts for the middle class and reestablishing abortion rights. As a former high school teacher he advocated for free school meals. Overall, a standup guy, however thirty years ago Jim was caught speeding in his automobile one night and was arrested for a DUI offense. Since then he swore off alcohol until now...

The Vice Presidential hopeful kicked open the front door. He greeted everyone before giving Jacqueline an endearing hug. Afterward, he raced over to the nearest beer keg and indulged. Many cups of beer and a few gropes later, Jim was inclined to go for a joyride. Jacqueline called, "Shotgun," before ordering some of the girls to go with them.

The secret service men were all high so they stayed behind. Mozz couldn't wait to get behind the wheel. An inebriated man of his stature had something to prove. Jim was confident that he could stay awake despite being so plastered. Responsible presidential candidates don't allow vice presidential candidates to drive drunk.

Regarding this particular case Barris did not care.

"You only live once and sometimes not that long," Barris thought to herself.

They all got inside of Mozz's car. The three girls that were sitting in the backseat screamed as Jim drove erratically down the street. He narrowly avoided crashing into parked cars. Jim's vehicle was approaching a speed of nearly 80 mph. Jacqueline lowered the passenger side window. She wished to feel the wind in her hair.

These little moments provided a rush that was exhilarating. Jim quickly approached a cross section where the traffic light turned red. Mozz stomped down on the brake. Two of the girls bumped their heads extremely hard on the seats in front of them. This resulted in instantaneous concussions, rendering these ladies unconscious.

The third girl was catapulted from the middle backseat and flew straight through the windshield. She landed on the curbside nearly forty feet away, but then rolled another fifteen feet before her body came to a complete halt. Her mangled corpse was wrapped around a telephone pole. Mozz and Jacqueline did one smart thing this evening and that involves observing safety laws by wearing their seatbelts. Barris giggled while tapping Mozz on the shoulder. Then they both got out of the automobile.

"Ha, ha, ha, ha, ha, ha. Last one back has to clean her up!" Barris exclaimed.

Jacqueline sprinted down the street while Jim stumbled behind. After that night, Mozz vowed to never take another sip of alcohol... until the next keg party.

U.S. Representative of Georgia Artemie Kramer Dean (AKD) is giving former President Dump a piggyback ride to one of his rallies because he's running late.

You're a true patriot, Artemie!

Don't worry Ronald I'll get you there on time!

Artemie,
You're still a big blonde, butch bitch, muscle bound and bound for Hell anus bleached and Crass, low class extramarital affair having Jezebel.

U.S Representative of Texas, Jolene Sprockett

Atlanta Rally

The stage was already set. Music blared at full volume as an introduction.

It ceased after former President, Ronald Dump stepped onto the stage and made his way to the podium. A typical outdoor venue for a Dump event with a few thousand people in attendance. Dump's constituents feverishly await the opening remarks of The Fuhrer.

Ronald straightened his tie and then spoke.

"Hello, to the great people of Georgia. I'm sure that every one of you realize that the radical Jacqueline Barris wants to destroy your livelihood and reduce America to a shadow of its former glory. She is a very nasty woman, very nasty. Personally, I don't like how she coordinates her outfits, just nasty. Jacqueline and 'President In-A Coma Triden' have an open border policy.

Illegal immigrants are coming in from dirty countries. I don't have to mention the immigrants coming in from Scandinavian Europe because that continent consists of good clean countries. If I were currently president, Russia never would've invaded Ukraine. Cassimir Lieutin is a wonderful man. He's just a little misunderstood.

He comes to my home in Florida once sometimes twice a week, gives the most soothing backrubs, and plows my plump buttocks very well. Such a generous lover. And to Jacqueline, is she black or Indian, who knows?

However, late at night I think of my nemesis. Then I beat my meat to the rhythm of a drum, or even bagpipes. I don't give a shit.

This does not change the fact that she's nasty. Very, very, nasty. There are turncoats in my own political party.

Senators that didn't support my claim on January 6th. I helped them get elected and that was how they repaid me. Now I will help them lose their seats.

The radical left is extremely upset because I overturned Roe vs. Wade.

Eventually, this country will reach the point where all abortions will become illegal. Slowly but surely. The right to choose should not exist, regardless of cases involving sexual assault.

A woman should be forced to give birth to that baby.

And every time she looks into the eyes of that infant, that woman can see a reflection of the man who raped her. Barris has a new running mate, Jim Mozz. This guy was arrested for a D.U.I. nearly thirty years ago.

He loves to say the word, weird. This and that is weird, weird, weird.

He tried to call me weird. I said, 'No, that's my VP selection. There isn't anything weird about me. E.D. Lance might have a furniture fetish but those are best kept secrets between a man and his décor'. I thank you," Dump said.

Then he gave a loud belch before stepping away from the podium.

Ronald was saluted with an overwhelming abundance of Sieg Heils while walking across the stage. This campaign is just starting to head into high gear.

Sofa Erotica

E.D Lance is arguably the most loathed and unpopular vice presidential candidate of the last fifteen years. He once vilified his own running mate by referring to him as the next Hitler waiting in the wings. Lance's desire to establish a nationwide ban on abortion makes him an enemy to the republic. This would effect women along with men that are positioned with power.

What happens when a government official accidentally gets his mistress pregnant? The wife might not approve of her husband's conduct. That "model citizen" doesn't want to struggle through the red tape. He'll want to acquire easy access to a confidential termination of pregnancy for his beloved harlot. Abortion is the only way to avoid a scandal and keep that political career on track.

Lance also believes that adults without children should have to pay higher taxes and have less voting rights. E.D. Lance categorically detests any woman that he identifies as a "childless cat lady". He believes that these individuals are miserable in life due to poor decisions that they made in life, and are adamant in creating an unbearable existence for those all around.

Within this perilous mind unspeakable thoughts roam. Therefore, E.D. Lance should be considered a menace.

Curiosity got the best of Ronald Dump's running mate. Lance became obsessed with U.S. Representative, Dana Omasio Cortell a.k.a. D.O.C. There was something about her that E.D. both despised and desired. For some inexplicable reason he couldn't fight his feelings toward the young congress woman.

On a Tuesday afternoon at approximately 2:00 pm Lance decided to pay Dana a visit. He was aware that Cortell was currently home, however he didn't have any intention of knocking on the front door.

E.D. tiptoed to the side of Dana's abode.

There is a significant distance between Cortell's house and those belonging to her neighbors. The closest being approximately 150 feet away. A very fortunate circumstance that benefited E.D. He found an old rusty bucket that was adjacent to the homestead. Lance proceeded to stand on top of it so that he could leer through one of the living room windows.

D.O.C. had just finished taking a shower. After drying off, Dana wrapped a large towel around her naked body. Subsequent to blow drying her hair, Dana entered the living room. Then she grabbed a book, sat down, and began to read. The truth is that E.D. Lance had very little interest in Dana per se. What D.O.C. was sitting on is a different matter.

Lance has a furniture fetish. Chairs, coffee tables, lamps, you name it. None of these pieces were more alluring to E.D. than Dana's living room sofa. Lance wrote an autobiography entitled: Redneck In Heat. He dedicated an entire chapter to his lust for furniture.

Some people thought Lance should've been institutionalized after the release of his book, but he only wanted to convey a message to the American people, 'Nothing can come between a man and his couch except this man... get it?'

Sweat trickled down E.D.'s face as his crazed eyes pierced through the window pane. Lance always pondered D.O.C.'s decorating style. The type of furnishings that she possessed. Now he had been made fully aware. Dana was heavily immersed in her reading. Completely oblivious to the prowler that stood before her living room window. E.D. sighed as he took in this glorious sight of D.O.C. sitting on the most lavish blue sofa. Every thread and seam of upholstery seemed to come together in order to present a small form of perfection. What a heavenly sight, indeed.

Lance found the manner in which D.O.C. leaned her body against one of the throw pillows, maddening.

"Don't be so rough. Put a some more care into your interaction. Caress, fluff, and hold it. A little foreplay will go a long way," E.D. thought to himself.

Lance unbuckled his belt then unzipped and lowered his pants ever so slightly. Before long, E.D. began to masturbate. Vigorously, I might add. The ethereal vision of this lean yet robust, well manufactured specimen was more than Lance could bear. It didn't take long for E.D. to ejaculate all over D.O.C.'s bed of petunias, and her cat that was wandering by. The feline hissed before scurrying away at full tilt with semen dripping from its tail.

This sound startled E.D. causing him to lose balance and fall off of the bucket. D.O.C. heard the commotion. She stood up from the couch and hurried over to the window and then opened it.

""Hey, who's out there?!" D.O.C. exclaimed.

After poking her head through the window, Dana could easily observe E.D. running down the road as he struggled to hold his pants up during the process.

Later that evening while lying in bed, E.D. fantasized about giving Dana's couch a "Golden Shower" right between the seat cushions. Lance knew that he could never return to the scene of his crime and lay eyes on that sofa again. He gripped his pillow in anger and great sorrow, indivisible.

E.D. wept quietly until he eventually fell asleep from his exhausting array of emotions.

The Whore Whisperer

The cross country touring has been going quite well, but Jacqueline Barris decided to grant herself a reprieve. She returned to Washington D.C. for one day of rest and relaxation at her favorite spa. After receiving an hour long massage, Jacqueline stood up from the table feeling reinvigorated. Suddenly an overhead rack of towels collapsed. One of the heavy planks of wood struck Jacqueline in the head.

The blow rendered her unconscious for a few minutes. A member of the secret service discovered Barris lying on the floor. Jacqueline awoke feeling rather discombobulated. The Vice President was quickly escorted to a private medical facility so that some tests could be conducted. Barris' doctor made the diagnosis that the Vice President had suffered a concussion, and getting some much needed rest was the best remedy.

A couple of days had passed. It turned out that the blow Barris suffered affected the frontal lobe of her brain. Somehow a most unusual ability has been unlocked in the form of telepathy. A magnificent gift such as this should never be bestowed upon a woman like

Jacqueline Barris. Apparently there is no time like the present to abuse it.

Once Barris learned of her newly acquired power she concocted a scheme to exact revenge against a couple of high profiled government officials that mocked her on a regular basis. There were a bevy of individuals that did exactly the same thing but Barris hated these two people in particular the most. One thing that Jacqueline's detractors have in common are an affinity for prostitutes. They frequently partake in spending quality time with hookers of the highest caliber. Jacqueline would now provide the talent with her own agenda in mind.

At any time or place Barris can take control of any person and bend them to her will. There wasn't any way to ascertain exactly how long this ability would last. Barris wanted to exploit this capability for all its worth, such as petty payback. Josh Mercer is the Governor of Maryland. He often accused jacqueline of having a weak progressive stance on crime during her tenure as district attorney.

On this very night while staying at the extravagant Lucindo Hotel, Mercer ordered a beautiful high end escort of Asian descent. Josh didn't hesitate to engage in debauchery as soon as his guest arrived. Jocelyn was the woman's name. Not the first time meeting with Mercer but it would be her last. She already was familiar with the routine.

Both Mercer and Jocelyn got undressed. Josh was into autoerotic asphyxiation. He gave his belt to Jocelyn before lying face down on the bed.The escort climbed on top of his back and gently wrapped the belt around Mercer's neck. She gradually increased the pressure.

Tightening the belt more and more. The safety word is, "potato". Josh felt immense pleasure as his eyes rolled to the back of his head. Almost another minute went by before the Governor barely squeaked out the word, po-tato. An evil grin formed on Jocelyn's face.

"I don't care if you say, 'French fry'. You're mashed potatoes, motherfucker!" Jocelyn exclaimed.

Then she completely tightened the belt around Mercer's neck. Jocelyn held on for dear life while Josh struggled to retain his own. In the end, Mercer ceased resisting after taking his final breath. Semen oozed from his lifeless corpse. Suddenly Jocelyn was released from Barris' mind control.

The young woman screamed before putting on her clothes and dashing out of the room in sheer panic.

Senator Louis Advern from the state of Ohio made claims that in the past Jacqueline Barris only became D.A. in the first place because of her connection to the former Mayor of San Francisco. Also, that she never finished law school. Barris despised Advern the most with his half cocked conspiracy theories. Louis is currently spending the weekend at a swanky resort just outside of Orlando, Florida with his mistress, Sandy. This woman happens to be a gold digger which is why she qualifies as a prostitute.

Jacqueline promptly used her mind control capabilities. Then Sandy insisted on Louis taking her to bed. They both disrobed soon after entering the bedroom. Some passionate kissing ensued, after which Louis got into bed. He didn't lay down, instead he was on all fours.

For a man that has denounced homosexuality and can only see it as abhorrent, he's certainly into a lot of "ass play". At first it started with a woman inserting a thumb or a couple of fingers. Now Advern has graduated to using dildos, or a partner utilizing a full strap on. You can always find the good Senator giddy with joy as long as he has something of significance up his butt. On average he has to make appointments to see his proctologist three or four times a month.

Sandy opened a drawer from the night stand. Then she reached inside before getting into bed, and positioning herself behind Louis. A few fingers were used for pleasure Advern before Sandy slipped a piece of cheese into his posterior. Louis was extremely satisfied with the effort that Sandy put forth. The level of ecstasy that Advern felt was grand but not as large as the jumbo size sewer rat Sandy attempted to shove up Louis' rectum.

The Senator took blows to the hit as his mistress beat

him severely with a five pound stainless steel vibrator. The rat was only half way in. Sandy did her best to force the rodent further up. The vermin vermin gnawed relentlesssly at Advern's cheese flavored colon. Louis sreamed in distress while the rodent attempted to feed even more so on the Senator's entrails.

Advern died shortly after, and it certainly wasn't due to a broken heart.

Sandy awakened from her hypnotic trance. Horrific gore became perceptible in full presentation. Blood spattered all over the sheets. Sandy's lover was dead with a rat hanging halfway out of his ass. It squeaked loudly as it frantically attempted to free itself from this old anus.

Sandy was consumed by disbelief but she correctly assumed that the authorities would implicate her in Advern's murder. The confused woman quickly got dressed, and gathered her luggage with a passport in hand. Then she headed straight to the airport. Jacqueline Barris soon discovered that after a couple of hours she no longer possessed the power of telepathy. Well, it was fun while it lasted.

38

My Rallies Are Bigger Than Yours

Atlanta, Georgia is where the venue is located. The time had come for Jacqueline Barris to prove that she could garner an even larger rally attendance than Ronald Dump, because she knew that would infuriate him to no end. Almost seven thousand people attended this particular assembly.

Jacqueline simply felt stupendous. She thought of herself as a well sought after rock star.

This was her moment. Barris wished to give the people what they desire the most, herself. After giving a ten minute speech that was completely devoid of any semblance of substance, Barris walked off of the backside of the platform. Moments later, a popular female rapper named Horsey Rider ran onto the stage. She picked up the microphone and muttered some gibberish. Then she began to talk about the importance of voting, and that our democracy is in imminent danger if Ronald Dump is re-elected.

Horsey conveyed her hope that this generation will make the right decision in order for the next one… hold that thought.

It was at this time that music started blaring and Horsey Rider began to rap. Apparently her biggest goal is to endorse twerking. She shook her buttocks rapidly, and made sure that all of the children in attendance could bear witness to this deplorable behavior because it is important to set an example.

Jacqueline applauded while Horsey continued to rap about riding men into the sunset for an additional fifteen minutes.

The rally literally became a circus. After Horsey Rider left the stage a clown riding a twelve ft. tall unicycle appeared. Several more performers juggling bowling pins came out on stage. This act was followed by a magician. His special trick was making everyone's precious time disappear.

A twister started walking among the crowd, making balloon animals for the kids. It is of the utmost importance that Jacqueline Barris spread a message of her competence by implementing viable economical policies and controlling inflation. There isn't anything that conveys this sentiment more efficiently than a twerking rapper, elephant rides, and free ice cream.

Barris' Political Rally

Entertaining her Constituents with
What She Sees her Constituents as...

Clowns!

Giving Back

Anger was the and only emotion that Ronald Dump Felt. Jacqueline Barris held rallies that were arguably larger than his. Everything about this is unacceptable. Ronald is the star of this show, and he couldn't allow anyone to shine brighter than himself. Everybody knew that he would've achieved an election landslide victory against Bo Triden, but now it won't be so easy to win back the presidency.

Palm Beach, Florida, inside of the most elegant mansion Dump began to cry and stomp his feet in protest.

"It's not fair. I want to win!" Ronald exclaimed.

Then he threw the remote control at his television. The impact created a large crack in the screen.

"Fradonnia, order a television! I broke another one!" Ronald shouted.

Dump's wife, Fradonnia entered the room.

"Why don't you stop throwing things at the t.v. then we won't need to buy more of them?" Fradonnia asked.

Ronald started to pout. He frowned while picking up

his pogo stick up from the floor. He used it to bounce up and down as he lashed out.

"Screw you, Fradonnia! My daughter is way hotter than you anyway! Just order the t.v. like I told you!" Ronald exclaimed.

Fradonnia stormed out of the living room with haste.

At that moment Dump's Campaign Manager, Pepper Jones entered the room. Ronald ceased the use of his pogo stick and placed it in the corner like a good little boy. In recent days, Pepper had become extremely concerned with Dump's increasingly idiosyncratic behavior. Late last night Dump demanded for Jones to come over and read him a bedtime story.

Pepper had to wait nearly forty-five minutes for someone to finally answer the front door. Ronald refused to do it himself because he was already wearing his pajamas and Fradonnia tucked him in already. A member of the secret service eventually answered the door and allowed Jones entry. Pepper was experiencing a large financial gain as Dump's campaign manager. Something as trivial as refusing to read Ronald a bedtime story could easily result in Jones' job termination.

Now there were more pressing matters. Pepper addressed the former President.

"Ronald, there has been a major social media backlash because of you making derogatory remarks about Jacqueline," Pepper said.

Ronald really didn't care. Lately his rival has been receiving much more media attention than himself. This creates the most unsettling reality for the former President, and we all know that Dump does not adhere to reality.

Pepper continued on, "It would be best to rebrand you. Distract the masses with a new story. Ronald the philanthropist. Your generosity and altruism will shine through," Jones said.

Dump frowned, "But I have none," Ronald said.

Pepper laughed, "It doesn't matter. We will create a brand new persona for you. A caring, modest humanitarian in the form of Ronald T. Dump," Pepper said. A sigh came forth from Ronald.

"This sounds totally lame," Ronald said. "I don't approve of all of this 'giving talk'. 'Taking' on the other hand..." Dump trailed off.

Pepper shook his head. "It is imperative that we get ahead of this thing, and force people to see you for something other than a hate monger. This is why I arranged it so tomorrow evening you'll be volunteering at a soup kitchen. Conveniently with a photo op, of course. You're going to help the homeless," Pepper said.

Dump rolled his eyes. "This will probably be a disaster but I'll do it. Not because of my heartfelt compassion. It's due to the fact that I'm majestic. I am a God among men. People look up to me.

They're all proud to be Americans because of everything that my administration has accomplished. Tomorrow night I will give back! Now go get my rubber ducky. I'm going to take a bath," Dump said.

The next evening, Ronald made his appearance at the Clearington Soup Kitchen. He was accompanied by a team from the secret service. Georgie Ronin runs this establishment. He gave instructions to Ronald and all of the other volunteers on how this operation will transpire. Ronald stood behind the food counter.

After the staff made proper preparations they were

ready to serve the homeless. Ronald instructed one of the secret service men to line his pockets with some of the free saltine crackers. Dump is quite fond of those and thought that a few would go well with the soup and sirloin steak that he planned to order from a posh five star restaurant later on. Ronald told another member of the secret service to grab some of the ham and turkey sandwiches and place them inside of a bag. The former Commander in Chief didn't have any intention of going home empty handed tonight.

A one armed war veteran attempted to introduce himself to the former President.

Dump smiled as he shook the veteran's hand, then he wiped his own hand off of his pants.

"Listen, I saw you a while ago and I had one of my men pick up a gift especially for you from a nearby department store. You are going to love it," Ronald said.

The former President presented the vet with the severed arm of a department store mannequin.

Ronald continued on, "Here you go. Just stick it in your shoulder socket like an action figure. I'm sure that there will be an adjustment period but then you'll be

47

perfectly fine. Thank you for your service," Dump said.

Then Ronald gave the disabled warrior a salute.

The veteran walked away with a plastic arm instead of a meal. He was so excited to meet the former President. Not anymore. Dump swatted away several of the homeless people due to poor hygiene. Ronald felt that if these transients would dare offend him with their odor, they were not worthy of receiving a meal.

The had to do better and give forth more effort next time. A bold vagabond approached Dump and told him that he voted for Triden during the last presidential election. These words infuriated Ronald. So the former Commander in Chief took the sandwich, bowl of soup, beverage, and small piece of beef that was intended for the Triden supporter and threw it all in the trash.

"Maybe next time you'll vote responsibly. Bye, bye," Dump said.

After everyone else was fed, Ronald ordered his men to escort the Triden supporter the hell out of there. The time had come for Dump to leave as well.

Before doing so, the former President took a few of the day old donuts that were meant to be served as dessert. Then he told everyone inside of the soup kitchen to vote for him and he thanked them for their continued support. One of the transients spat on the floor in response.

Dump shook his head in disgust.

"That's why you're poor and I'll leave you to it," Ronald said.

This evening served as quite a learning experience for Dump. He realized that he was far from being altruistic. The former President tried but failed miserably, although he did spend quality time with the "have nots". Dump promptly got inside of his limousine.

A return to this pampered, sheltered life is all that Ronald could ever ask for... and world domination.

Dye Doesn't Lie

Weeks had gone by. Former President, Ronald Dump was frantic. His rival Jacqueline Barris continued to attract larger rallies than him, and she continued to rise in the polls. A news story broke about Dump's volunteer work at the Clearington Soup Kitchen and it was not good. Whoever said, Any publicity is good publicity didn't have this material to work with.

Everyone seemed to be talking about Dump depriving some of the homeless people of meals, stealing food for himself, and the unintentional mocking of a disabled U.S. War Veteran. Ronald was at a loss. What could he possibly do? The ex- President desperately craved advice. With very few available options, Dump recently got in touch with an old friend.

This individual is expected to make an appearance at Ronald's estate at any moment now. Suddenly the doorbell rang. Within a minute, Ronald's butler, Charles entered the room along with a guest.

"Sir, may I present the man that once served as consigliere to the Dump crime family, 'The People's Mayor' and your former personal attorney, Mr. Rudy Boobieani?" Charles said.

Then he left the two men alone in the living room. Ronald greeted his old friend, and then they sat down in a couple of chairs. Dump was distraught and didn't know where else to turn, but whenever in need of not so- sound advice in the form of incoherent gibberish he needn't look any further. Boobiani had been under the hot Florida sun for a long period of time. Despite sitting indoors now, he was sweating quite profusely. The brand new hair dye that Boobiani applied this morning was beginning to run down both sides of his face. Rudy pulled a handkerchief out of the pocket of his suit.

He subtly dabbed at the liquid running off of his scalp.

Then he spoke, "Ronald, I'm glad that you reached out. It's been a long time. Sorry to hear about your troubles. Not that long ago I had some very serious legal troubles and no one bothered to check on me, but that's all in the past even though I've been indicted and the investigation is ongoing. I told them that I didn't want to investigate Bo Triden. Yes, they should investigate Bo Triden.

Hey Ronnie, do you remember when I showed up for that interview with a half shaven head? People were going wild," Rudy said.

Ronald started to respong but he was sharply cut off.

"Wait a minute, damn it!" Rudy said. "Let me finish. I'm lawyer."

Ronald remained silent while Boobiani dabbed at his face with what is now a soaking wet handkerchief. The more Rudy talked the more black ooze spilled from his head.

Rudy rambled on, "I always thought that we should sue members of congress. A grand injustice has taken place. I stayed at the Beverly Lights Hotel and they didn't have the decency to provide a continental breakfast. The hell with modern technology. After washing my clothes, the maid places my underpants on a clothesline. That way they can air dry like God intended.

Of course this proves that there wasn't any fraud committed. You were always an ethical and reasonable client. I remember before taking your case the suggestion that you made for everyone to inject themselves with a disinfectant in order to kill the Covid Virus inside of us. That was ingenious. I said to myself, 'This man is a visionary. He should have a P.H.D. in being awesome!'

I will tear up all letters from Congress on your behalf," Rudy said.

At this point the hair dye ran down both sides of Boobiani's face. His suit, tie and shirt were also covered with the black substance. It was as if someone left the bathwater running, and no one is at home to turn it off.

Rudy stood up from his seat. He used his sleeve to clear away some of the dye from his face.

Rudy continued on, "We'll take this all the way to the Supreme Court if I deem it necessary. I have yet to be disbarred in all 50 states. Keep in mind that they can never disbar my heart. My God, I ate three hardboiled eggs this morning and for the life of me I still can't take a shit. This is a travesty!" Rudy declared.

Finally, Ronald stood up from his chair while grinning.

"Well, it's been nice catching up but you have to go. More than one insane person involved in the election process is overkill. You can take my case to Bellevue if you like. As for now, get the hell out of here, Rudy!

Your hair is dripping all over my carpet!" Dump exclaimed. Boobiani mumbled to himself as he vacated the premises.

Rudy Boobiani's
hair dye malfunction
It's dripping everywhere.

More paper towels, more!
I can't Stop Sweating!
Help Me !!

In the process Rudy left a trail of black hair dye all across the living room carpet and exotic hardwood floor that led to the front door. Suddenly Ronald had an epiphany. Dump came to the conclusion that the only advice that he would ever require is from himself. When the former President was still in office he never listened the advice of his chief of staff, military strategists, or any sane individual with credentials.

Advice is something that Dump never heeded in the past and he's not going to start now. Ronald regained all of his self confidence. He is now prepared, more than ever (which is still not at all). Ronald smirked before grimacing at the floor."Charles, come here!" Dump exclaimed. "...And bring the mop!"

Prelude To The Presidential Debate

Tuesday night in Philadelphia at a deluxe town hall is where the two presidential candidates gathered. Hester Malt has taken the role of tonight's moderator. The venue for this historic event has reached full capacity. It couldn't possibly accommodate a single additional person. The spectators were plentiful, and reporters from a vast number of news outlets were present as well.

Uproarious applause filled the toen hall as Jacqueline Barris and her opponent Ronald T. Dump walked out onto the stage. They reluctantly shook hands with each other before strolling to their set podiums. Hester Malt explained the rules of the debate and had every intention of enforcing them.

"The first question..." Hester said before an abrupt interruption.

Presidential Debate - The Musical

Ronald-

♪ Jackie, first you are an Indian then you say ♪
♪you're Jamaican♪

Jacqueline-

♪ Hey Fatboy, do you really need to eat another ♪
♪piece of bacon?♪

Ronald-

♪ You think I'm not qualified?/ ♪

Jacqueline-

♪You've never acknowledged global warming/ ♪
♪ You'll just take a sunbath♪

Ronald-

♪ No, for that I have a tanning booth, ♪
♪ although there will be Nafta reform♪

Jacqueline-

♪You'll be indicted again before dinner/ ♪

♪ *It's still not the biggest wave before the storm* ♪

Ronald-

♪ *You're dumb as rocks and* ♪
♪ *you can't keep your head above water* ♪

Jacqueline-
♪ *Take a shower/ That'll give you a chance* ♪
♪ *to fantasize about your own daughter* ♪

Ronald & Jacqueline-

♪ *Hey Moderator, Shut the fuck up!* ♪

♪ *You can stick all of your questions right up your greasy* ♪
♪ *butt We have taken over/ This much is true* ♪
♪ *We're talking over you, so what are you going to do?* ♪

-

♪ *Tell your running mate, Jim to pull the tampon* ♪
♪ *out of his twat* ♪

Jacqueline-

♪ *I heard E.D. Lance dry humped an ottoman* ♪
♪ *but then he got caught* ♪

Ronald-

♪ *Ah, a critical communist from the far radical left* ♪

Jacqueline-

♪ Keep talking out of the back of your ass/♪
♪That's what you do best♪

Ronald-

♪You're giving migrant criminals and♪
♪ mental patients green cards/♪
♪Fulfilling dreams and hopes♪

Jacqueline-

♪Leave them out of this/ I'm busy pandering for their votes♪

Ronald-

♪You don't have any patriotism or morals/♪
♪Not even an ounce♪

Jacqueline-

♪This coming from someone convicted of business fraud♪
♪on 34 counts♪

Jacqueline & Ronald-

♪Hey moderator, shut the fuck up!♪

♪You can stick all of your questions right up your greasy♪
♪ butt We have taken over/ This much is true♪
♪We're talking over you, so what are you going to do?♪

Ronald-

♪ Project 2025 is the future/ ♪
♪ Creating what will be the norm ♪

Jacqueline-

♪ You're the poster child for Roe Vs. Wade/ Should've never ♪
♪ been born ♪

Ronald-

♪ I'm the leader of men/ A primary example ♪

Jacqueline-

♪ Of a walking, talking, piece of shit/ ♪
♪ Merely a stool sample ♪

Ronald-

♪ Do me a favor, don't grin/ ♪
♪ You're a clucking, cackling hen ♪

Jacqueline-

♪ In your case, public speaking should be considered ♪
♪ an unforgivable sin ♪

Ronald-

♪ You're a nasty witch with a feminine itch/ ♪
♪ Is it Gonorrhea? ♪

Jacqueline-

♪*Every word out of your mouth is pure diarrhea*♪

Ronald & Jacqueline-

♪*Hey moderator, shut the fuck up!*♪
♪*You can stick all of your questions right up your greasy* ♪
♪*butt We have taken over/ This much is true*♪
♪*We're talking over you, so what are you going to do...?*♪

There wasn't much left to say. The debate ended and some of the restless spectators decided to attack Hester Malt. He was criticized for being a terrible moderator before being blugeoned by several attendees with folding chairs. Chaos from the crowd ensued. Jacqueline and Ronald stared at each other with deep seeded hatred in their eyes...

Mortal Combat

The stage was set with the podiums pushed aside. The two presidential candidates ran across the stage and lunged toward each other. Jacqueline landed a couple of punches before Dump sidekicked her in the stomach. That devastating blow sent the Vice President spiraling to the floor.

"Na, na, can't catch me, bitch," Ronald said.

Then he ran out of the town hall. Jacqueline got back on her feet. She knew that the time had come to finish this once and for all. Barris ran outside of the town hall in pursuit of Dump. The Vice President entered the back alley. Barris smelled a rat.

So naturally she could feel Dump's presence despite not having any visual confirmation. Barris leaped over a large puddle of urine. Without warning, Ronald emerged from behind a dumpster. He cracked Jacqueline in the head with a rusty tire iron. This caused Barris to spin around in bewilderment.

The backdoor to one of the buildings had been left ajar. Dump ran inside and made his way up to the third floor. Before he could turn the knob of the entrance door, Jacqueline seemingly materialized out of nowhere. She delivered a spin kick that sent Dump face first into the wall (A big beautiful wall). The impact caused Ronald to drop the tireiron.

Then the Vice President brought forth a flurry of punches to Dump's face, abdomen, and chest. The former President delivered a head butt to Barris' face. Suddenly, a crimson colored illumination burned brightly in Ronald's eyes.

"Grab her by the pussy! Grab her by the pussy!" Dump bellowed.

The devil instructed him to do it and he did. Ronald distracted Barris by stomping on her foot. Then he latched on to Jacqueline's crotch, and proceeded to drag her down three flights of stairs. Barris hollered in torment the entire time before being thrown out of the building's backdoor. Despite hitting the ground with immense force, Jacqueline got up immediately and ran her sore vagina right out of that alleyway.

Ronald chased after her like a mad man. Through sheer willpower, Jacqueline managed to jog vigorously for five blocks while suffering from exhaustion. Finally she reached Manson Hardware, panting and out of breath. This store is part of the nation's largest hardware chain. Barris assumed that somewhere inside of this establishment she would find vital tools capable of helping her end this rivalry for good.

Before Barris could turn her head, she was hit from behind and fell backward into a speeding shopping cart. The person pushing it was none other than Ronald Dump. He ran swiftly down the aisle before letting go. The cart sped up to the highest velocity before crashing into one of the kitchen counter models. The Vice President screamed right before impact. The shopping cart flipped to its side.

Barris dragged herself out, and then traversed a different aisle. Ronald suddenly appeared in front of her. He smiled while keeping his hands behind his back. One of the store's sales associates approached Barris from behind. He asked Jacqueline if she needed any help finding products.

Unexpectedly, Dump swung a shovel at Barris. Thanks to some extremely fast reflexes she just barely ducked in time. The sales associate that was standing in close proximity lacked the Vice President's finesse and agility. He was instantly decapitated. Jacqueline vacated the aisle before the severed head hit the floor.

The power tools section is exactly what Barris was searching for.

She picked up one of the display nail guns and filled it with ammunition. Now she was ready to play. Dump picked up a pair of hedge clippers but he dropped them after Barris started firing the gun. Nails shot out at Ronald in rapid repetition.

The Vice President had plenty to smile about now. "I'm literally going to nail your water buffalo ass," Jacqueline said. "Ha, ha, ha, ha, ha, ha."

Ronald ran for cover, in and out of numerous aisles. Eventually, Barris caught up to Ronald in the section containing chemical products. The Vice President stood six feet away while directing the nailgun toward her rival's head. Dump placed his hand on top of a large container that was sitting on one of the shelves.

He subtly unscrewed and removed the cap. A store sales associate named Jen approached Jacqueline from the side.

"Ma'am, I'm afraid I'll have to ask you to put that down. We can't afford to have any horseplay inside of the store, even if you are second in command to the leader of the free world," Jen said.

Ronald crept closer to Jacqueline while the sales associate spoke. Within an instant, Dump flung the contents of the container at Jacqueline.

Fortunately for the Vice President, Dump's aim was poor. This in turn happened to be extremely unfortunate for Jen. Barris was already on the move before Jen became completely drenched with the hazardous compound.

The chemical in question turned out to be nitric acid. Immediately after contact, flesh began to melt off of Jen's skull in the same manner that ice cream drips off of a cone when its been exposed to the sun for an extended period of time.

The woman could only release shrills for an extraordinarily short duration. Under the circumstances it could be said that she developed an instant speech impediment. Dump entered another aisle and Jacqueline followed suit.

She had him at point blank range. Ronald stopped in his tracks. He turned to face his rival while breathing heavily. Jacqueline approached Dump and pressed the barrel of the nailgun against his forehead. Barris smiled as she pulled the trigger.

In an instant that vibrant smile disappeared. Jacqueline was out of ammunition. Now a grin crawled across Ronald's face. He hit the Vice President in her throat before running once again. Barris collapsed on the floor as she gasped for air. About twenty seconds passed before Jacqueline got back on her feet.

Her resilience and persistence is second to none. Dump vacated the premises at a brisk, break neck speed. Once again, Jacqueline pursued her nemesis. Ronald jolted down the street, passing a museum as Barris closed in on the former President. A pregnant woman stood in the middle of the sidewalk.

Dump shoved the unsuspecting, expectant mother out of his way. Greta went tumbling down a long flight of stairs made of stone. Subsequent to her hitting the ground, her stomach burst open like a watermelon. The contents of this woman's belly were strewn about. A flock of seagulls swooped down and fed upon remnants of the unborn fetus.

I suppose that she "re Greta" coming into contact with Dump on this day. Meanwhile, Jacqueline was in close proximity of Ronald. She leapt toward Dump and tackled him to the ground. They both got up and began trading punches again. Jacqueline performed an axe kick, landing on top of Dump's head.

Pregnant
This Woman met former
President Dump and didn't
get the right to choose.

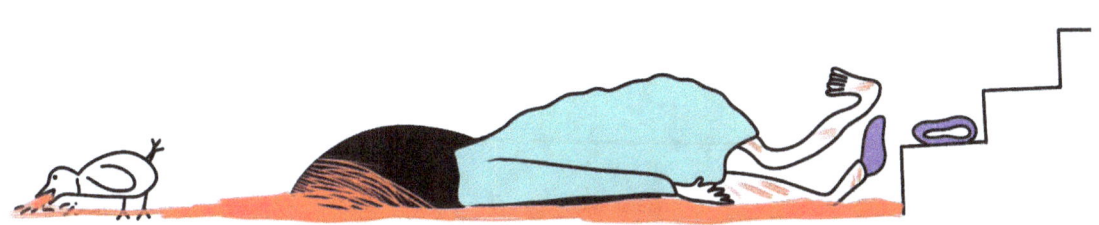

He grunted in pain as the fight moved out into the middle of a street with heavy traffic.

Ronald stepped to the side and landed a low kick that shattered Jacqueline's left knee. She bellowed and attempted to limp before returning with a palm strike that completely obliterated Ronald's nose. This devastating blow caused Dump to holler. His affliction was tremendous and he bled quite profusely.

Both of these candidates reveled in their hostility. They faced each other and prepared themselves for what would be the final blow...

Taking A Time Out

Pleasantville Hospital had only one dual, coed patient room available.

Both Jacqueline Barris and Ronald T. Dump were forced to share it. There were curtain dividers provided to ensure privacy. Of course it didn't matter. These two bedridden patients did not wish to exist in the same zip code with one another, let alone sharing the same room.

It turns out that having an actual street brawl in the middle of the road is never ideal. They were both hit and nearly killed by a man driving a large semi- trailer truck. A substantial amount of recovery time is required before either one of these "exemplary" world leaders can make a return to the campaign trail. The curtains are currrently open because a special guest has been sched-uled for a visit.

An assigned nurse named Renee entered the room. A young woman that possessed unparalleled beauty. Dump desired to grab her by the pussy, alas both of his arms are broken. The nurse smiled before making an announcement.

"May I present our benevolent President Of The United States, Bo Triden!" Renee exclaimed.

Then she quickly stepped to the side and allowed Triden and his secret service men access the room. Ronald rolled his eyes with contempt. The grin on Jacqueline's face quickly faded. Bo seemed to be filled with glee. He was most pleased to spend time with dear old friends. Unfortunately, he wouldn't find any here. "How are you doing, kiddos?" Bo asked.

Before either patient could respond, Bo continued on, "Here's the thing, Jackie, I know that you have a little rebellious streak in you but it needs to be tamed. Ronald, you're an awful human being. It is set in stone that you'll burn in Hell for all of eternity, end of story," President Triden said.

Dump countered, "Bo, shouldn't you still be in bed? It's 3:00 in the afternoon, nap time," Ronald retorted.

"What do you know, sucka?" President Triden asked. ""As a matter of fact, let me tell you about Corn Starch. That dude was incorrigible, man. He broke into many houses in our neighborhood. Stealing every box of breakfast cereal he could find.

If he came across healthy cereal that was rich in fiber he'd take that too. Why? We were all kids. None of us wanted to eat that shit. At the time we were capable of having regular bowel movements without the assistance of natural laxatives, no problem.

But Corn Starch wanted to show all of the neighborhood kids, who's the baddest. One day I approached him on the street and I said, 'Look man, you're not going to do this anymore. We won't stand for it. You can either take us all on and lose, or we can eat cereal together in solidarity.'

A single tear fell from his eye. He apologized before we hugged it out, because breakfast is the most important meal of the day. Am I getting through to you all? There is a vital moral to this story that you must heed," Bo said.

Both Dump and Barris glanced at each other before turning their attention back toward Bo. They simultaneously hurled insults at the President and then told him to get the hell out.

Triden frowned before speaking, "Ronald Dump you're simply despicable. Did you know I was going to allow you to rub my wet leg hair down in the sun. Then there is the opportunity to watch it curl back up, but now I revoke such a privilege," Triden said.

Ronald cleared his throat.

"I think I'll get over it, Bo," Dump said. Triden turned to face Jacqueline.

"As for you, Missy, keep your mouth shut! You still work for me," President Triden said.

A smug grin appeared on Jacqueline's face.

"Not for long, asshole," Barris said. "Ha, ha, ha, ha, ha, ha, ha, ha!"

Epilogue

In November of this year these two titans will square off in an election of a lifetime that will determine our fate for the foreseeable future and far beyond. Are either of these candidates qualified to run the country?

Ultimately, that is for you to decide. Vote for the one you prefer. Vote for the lesser of two evils.

Regardless of your position, be certain to cast your vote or don't complain later. Of course the antiquated electoral college voting system has yet to be abolished, so does your vote truly matter at all?

In reality, no matter which candidate emerges victorious... We all lose. Ciao!

Sean Seville is an author/entertainer from
Chicago,Illinois.